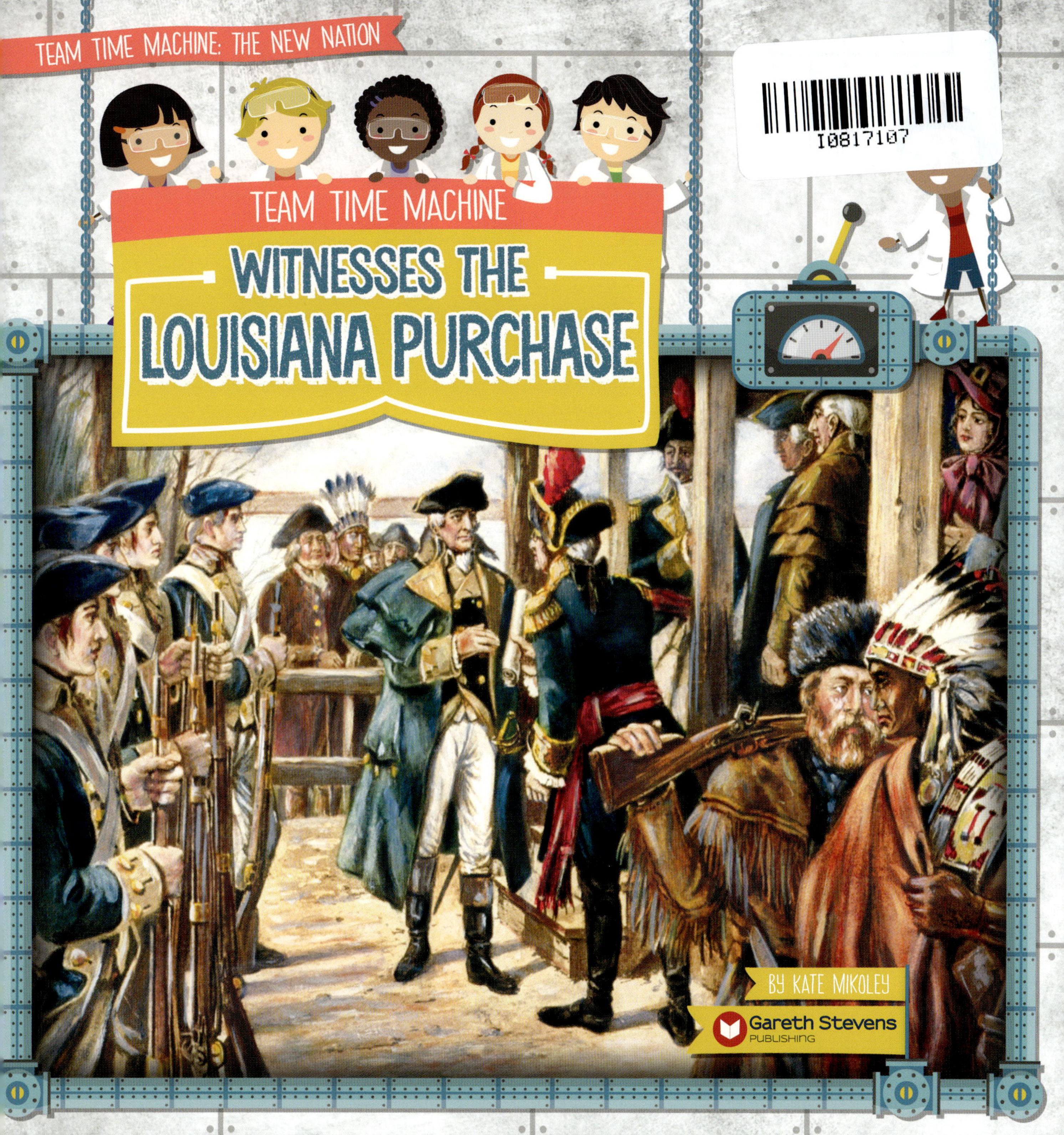
TEAM TIME MACHINE: THE NEW NATION
TEAM TIME MACHINE
WITNESSES THE
LOUISIANA PURCHASE
BY KATE MIKOLEY
Gareth Stevens
PUBLISHING

Please visit our website, www.garethstevens.com. For a free color catalog of all our high-quality books, call toll free 1-800-542-2595 or fax 1-877-542-2596.

Library of Congress Cataloging-in-Publication Data

Names: Mikoley, Kate, author.
Title: Team Time Machine witnesses the Louisiana Purchase / Kate Mikoley.
Description: New York : Gareth Stevens Publishing, 2021. | Series: Team Time Machine: The New Nation | Includes index.
Identifiers: LCCN 2020005487 | ISBN 9781538257098 (library binding) | ISBN 9781538257074 (paperback) | ISBN 9781538257081 | ISBN 9781538257104 (ebook)
Subjects: LCSH: Louisiana Purchase–Juvenile literature. | United States–History–1801-1809–Juvenile literature.
Classification: LCC E333 .M54 2020 | DDC 973.4/6-dc23
LC record available at https://lccn.loc.gov/2020005487

First Edition

Published in 2021 by
Gareth Stevens Publishing
111 East 14th Street, Suite 349
New York, NY 10003

Designer: Katelyn E. Reynolds
Editor: Therese Shea

Photo credits: Cover, pp. 1, 15 (main), 19, 23 (main), 29 Bettmann/Getty Images; cover, pp. 1–24 (series characters) Lorelyn Medina/Shutterstock.com; cover, pp. 1–24 (time machine elements) Agor2012/Shutterstock.com; cover, pp. 1–24 (background texture) somen/Shutterstock.com; p. 5 MPI/Getty Images; p. 7 Artindo/Shutterstock.com; p. 9 (main) pavalena/Shutterstock.com; p. 9 (inset) Nawrocki/ClassicStock/Getty Images; p. 11 (main), 13 DeAgostini/Getty Images; p. 11 (inset) GraphicaArtis/Getty Images; p. 15 (inset) Snyde/Shutterstock.com; p. 17 Scott Olson/Getty Images; p. 21 Robert Alexander/Getty Images; p. 23 (inset) courtesy of the Library of Congress; p. 25 PhotoQuest/Getty Images; p. 27 Everett Collection Historical/Alamy Stock Photo.

Printed in the United States of America

Some of the images in this book illustrate individuals who are models. The depictions do not imply actual situations or events.

CPSIA compliance information: Batch #CS20GS: For further information contact Gareth Stevens, New York, New York at 1-800-542-2595.

CONTENTS

WORDS IN THE GLOSSARY APPEAR IN **BOLD** TYPE THE FIRST TIME THEY ARE USED IN THE TEXT.

CHAPTER 1: A BIG PURCHASE

"I'm so happy it's the weekend!" Mia said. She slid her backpack over her shoulder.

"Me too," agreed Ben. "I'm going to visit my grandma. She just bought a new house. It's twice as big as her old one!"

"That's kind of like the Louisiana Purchase!" Sam said.

Mia and Ben both turned to Sam with puzzled looks on their faces.

"The Louisiana Purchase doubled the size of the United States," Sam explained. "Ben's grandma doubled the size of her house with a purchase!"

MEET TEAM TIME MACHINE

TEAM TIME MACHINE IS A GROUP OF FRIENDS WHO FOUND A TIME MACHINE ONE DAY IN A VERY ODD LIBRARY. THEY DISCOVERED THAT BOOKS FROM THE LIBRARY COULD POWER THE MACHINE AND TRANSPORT THEM TO DIFFERENT PLACES AND TIMES. IN THIS ADVENTURE, MIA, BEN, AND SAM WITNESS THE LOUISIANA PURCHASE!

IN 1803, THE LOUISIANA PURCHASE ADDED 828,000 SQUARE MILES (2,144,510 SQ KM) OF LAND TO THE UNITED STATES.

A GROWING NATION

"Oh yeah," Mia replied. "When was that again?"

"I don't remember," Sam replied. "I guess we all could use a reminder."

"To the library!" the trio shouted.

At the library, the friends searched for a book on the Louisiana Purchase.

"Found one!" said Ben, opening a yellow book. "The Louisiana Purchase **treaty** was signed in 1803," he read.

"Let's go," Mia said. Ben slid the book into an opening in the time machine and pulled the handle.

THE LOUISIANA PURCHASE HAD TO DO WITH LAND BOUGHT BY THE UNITED STATES FROM FRANCE. FRANCE HAD **ACQUIRED** THE LAND FROM SPAIN.
FRANCE
SPAIN

CHAPTER 2: A LOOK AT THE LAND

On the journey back in time, the team recalled what they knew about the Louisiana Purchase. In 1803, France owned the Louisiana Territory, which included the Mississippi River and New Orleans, an important port.

"Why did the United States need to buy the land?" Mia wondered.

"Before France owned the territory, Spain had," Sam replied. "Spain let the United States use the Mississippi River and New Orleans for **commerce**. When France got the land, Americans weren't sure France would let them use the river and port."

THE LOUISIANA TERRITORY WAS MUCH BIGGER THAN WHAT'S KNOWN AS LOUISIANA TODAY. IT COVERED THE LAND BETWEEN THE ROCKY MOUNTAINS AND THE MISSISSIPPI RIVER.

AMERICANS USED THE MISSISSIPPI RIVER FOR TRANSPORTATION AND TRADE.
MISSISSIPPI RIVER
NEW ORLEANS

CHAPTER 3: PARIS

Finally, the team arrived. They looked at the date on the time machine. They'd reached April 12, 1803.

"We're too early!" Ben cried.

"No, it's perfect!" Sam said. "This is the day James Monroe got to Paris, France."

As they stepped out of the library, they saw that it now looked like a shop in Paris. On the busy street, Mia spotted a tall man hurrying along. It was James Monroe! The trio set off, hiding in the crowd as they ran after Monroe.

PRESIDENT THOMAS JEFFERSON SENT JAMES MONROE TO PARIS TO PURCHASE LAND FOR THE UNITED STATES FROM FRANCE.

JAMES MONROE WOULD BECOME U.S. PRESIDENT IN 1817.

CHAPTER 4: LIVINGSTON AND MONROE MEET

Monroe walked to a park and stopped. Mia, Ben, and Sam stopped too. They ducked behind a wall. Monroe shook hands with another man he called Robert.

"That must be Robert Livingston, the U.S. **minister** to France," Mia said.

The men talked. Livingston had wanted to work out a deal with the French to purchase New Orleans for the United States. To do this, he had needed to meet with a French official named Charles-Maurice de Talleyrand. Livingston spent months trying to get in contact with Talleyrand.

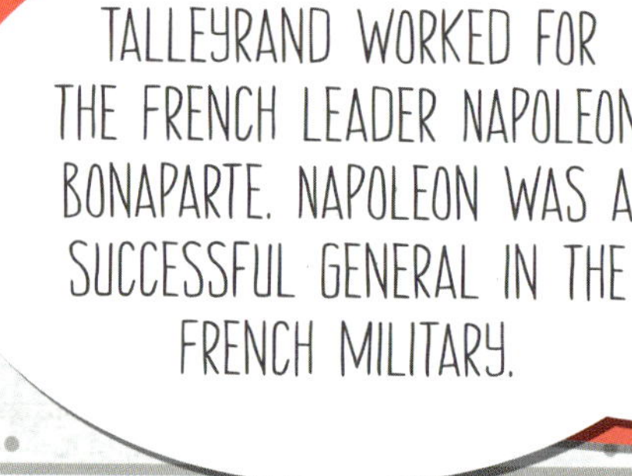

IN 1804, THE YEAR AFTER THE LOUISIANA PURCHASE, NAPOLEON MADE HIMSELF **EMPEROR** OF FRANCE.

Finally, Robert Livingston said, he spoke with Talleyrand. The kids listened as he told Monroe what happened just one day earlier. Talleyrand said Napoleon wanted to sell the entire Louisiana Territory.

"The whole territory?!" Ben shouted.

"Shhh!" Mia whispered. "They'll hear you!"

Livingston explained to Monroe that France needed the money because of costly wars. The French were also worried Great Britain might capture the land anyway. Napoleon decided it made more sense to sell the territory.

AMERICANS WEREN'T EXPECTING FRANCE TO SELL THE ENTIRE TERRITORY. MONROE AND LIVINGSTON HAD TO DECIDE WHAT TO DO QUICKLY.

AROUND THIS TIME, THE FRENCH WERE LOSING CONTROL OF THE LAND NOW KNOWN AS HAITI. THEIR EFFORTS TO STOP A **REVOLUTION** THERE HAD FAILED. WITHOUT THIS LAND, NAPOLEON AND OTHER FRENCH LEADERS DIDN'T THINK LOUISIANA WOULD BE AS IMPORTANT TO THEM.

Monroe seemed as surprised as Ben to hear Napoleon was offering the whole Louisiana Territory. Jefferson had asked him to first try to buy New Orleans and territory in today's Florida. If he couldn't, his goal was to reach an agreement allowing the United States to continue using the Mississippi River and the port at New Orleans.

The friends watched as Monroe's serious face lit up. His **negotiations** wouldn't be as hard as he'd expected.

IN ADDITION TO ALLOWING TRADE TO CONTINUE, THE LOUISIANA PURCHASE WOULD GIVE THE PEOPLE OF THE UNITED STATES MORE LAND FOR FARMING.

CHAPTER 6: NEGOTIATIONS

Monroe and Livingston set off down the street. The two men had to start negotiating a price with French officials, including Charles-Maurice de Talleyrand. Jefferson had told Monroe he could use up to $10 million to buy territory. But now much more land was being offered, and that would likely cost more.

The American officials had months of negotiations ahead. Luckily, Team Time Machine could use their time machine to travel forward in time too! They headed back to the library.

MONROE AND LIVINGSTON COULDN'T CALL THE UNITED STATES FOR **PERMISSION** TO BUY LOUISIANA—PHONES DIDN'T EXIST YET! AND SENDING MESSAGES OVERSEAS TOOK A LOT OF TIME. THEY HAD TO MAKE THE DECISION THEMSELVES.

MONROE (LEFT) AND LIVINGSTON (MIDDLE) ARE SHOWN HERE NEGOTIATING THE DEAL WITH CHARLES-MAURICE DE TALLEYRAND.

CHAPTER 7: THE TREATY

The kids placed a special bookmark in their book and put it back in the machine. They traveled to May 2, 1803. When they stepped out of the library, they found themselves in an office. They ducked behind a desk just as a group of men entered the room. They recognized James Monroe and Robert Livingston. Another French official was introduced to the men as François Barbé-Marbois.

As the men talked and looked at maps, the kids heard them strike a deal for $15 million.

THE UNITED STATES PAID $15 MILLION FOR THE WHOLE LOUISIANA TERRITORY—ONLY $5 MILLION MORE THAN THEY PLANNED TO SPEND ON JUST NEW ORLEANS AND FLORIDA!

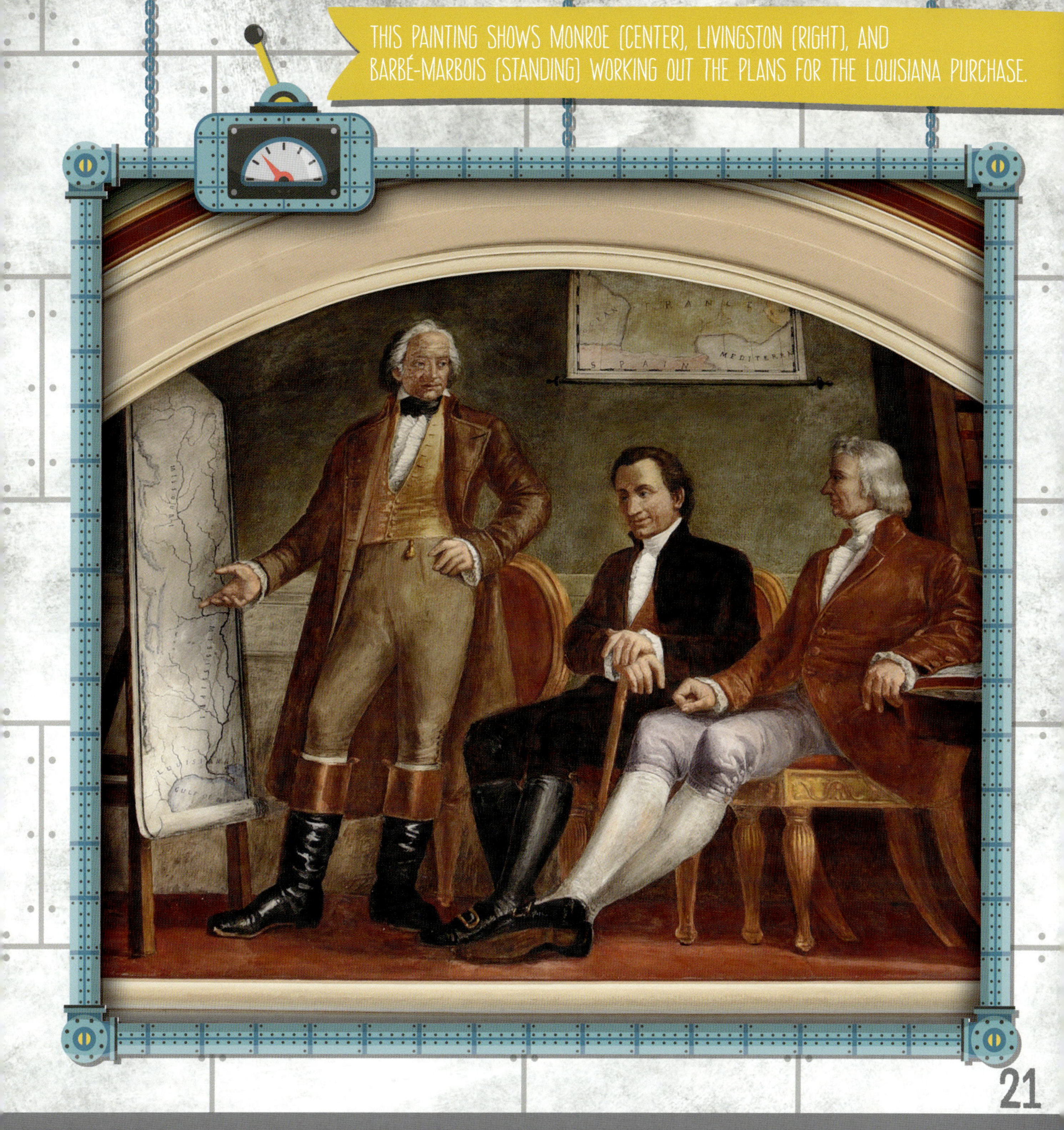

THIS PAINTING SHOWS MONROE (CENTER), LIVINGSTON (RIGHT), AND BARBÉ-MARBOIS (STANDING) WORKING OUT THE PLANS FOR THE LOUISIANA PURCHASE.

Mia, Ben, and Sam watched as the men signed the treaty that would be remembered as the greatest land deal in U.S. history. But even as they were signing it, the men didn't know exactly what they were buying.

The treaty said the United States would get the Louisiana Territory that France had received from Spain. The exact **boundaries** were unclear, though. Still, the men knew they had made a great deal and signed the treaty.

IN THIS IMAGE, LIVINGSTON SHAKES BARBÉ-MARBOIS'S HAND WHILE MONROE SIGNS THE LOUISIANA PURCHASE TREATY.

A Convention between the French republick and the United States of America.

The first consul of the French republick in the name of the French people, and the President of the United States of America, having by a treaty bearing date on this day terminated all differences relative to Louisiana and established on a solid foundation the friendship which unites the two nations, and wishing in conformity with the 2d and 5th articles of the convention of the 8th Vendre 9th year of the French republick, 30th of Sept. 1800, to secure the payment of the sums due by France to the citizens of the U. States, have respectively nominated as plenipotentiaries, that is to say, the first Consul in the name of the French people, the citizen Francis Barbé Marbois minister of the publick treasury and the President of the U. States of America by & with the advice and consent of their senate, Robt. R. Livingston minister plenipotentiary of the said States and James Monroe minister plenipotentiary and Envoy Extraordinary of the said States near the government of the French republick, who after having exchanged their full powers have agreed to the following articles.

Art: 1.

JAMES MONROE WROTE THIS **DRAFT** OF THE LOUISIANA PURCHASE TREATY.

CHAPTER 8: IS IT CONSTITUTIONAL?

As the men left the room, Sam said, "One more stop, team!"

The kids used the time machine again. This time, it took them to October 20, 1803. The kids entered a room filled with men. It was the room where the U.S. Senate met. A few senators were arguing about whether the Louisiana Purchase was constitutional, or allowed by the **Constitution**.

After a while, the Senate voted. There were 24 votes approving it and 7 against it. That was enough to ratify, or approve, the treaty.

EVEN THOMAS JEFFERSON WASN'T SURE IF THE TREATY WAS CONSTITUTIONAL. THE U.S. CONSTITUTION DIDN'T CLEARLY STATE THAT THE GOVERNMENT COULD BUY NEW LAND.

THIS IS WHAT THE U.S. CAPITOL LOOKED LIKE WHEN THE SENATE VOTED ON THE LOUISIANA PURCHASE TREATY.

CHAPTER 9: MAKING SENSE OF THE MONEY

As the friends walked back to the library, Mia flipped through the Louisiana Purchase book. She found what she was looking for as she stepped inside.

"I thought $15 million sounded like a lot of money," she told her friends. "But it says here that was less than 3 cents an acre. That *is* a good deal!"

"It's weird to imagine what the country would look like if it wasn't for the Louisiana Purchase," Ben added.

IN TODAY'S MONEY, THE $15 MILLION SPENT ON THE LOUISIANA PURCHASE WOULD EQUAL ABOUT $340 MILLION.

THE LOUISIANA TERRITORY OFFICIALLY BECAME PART OF THE UNITED STATES ON MARCH 10, 1804. THIS PAINTING SHOWS THE **CELEBRATION** THAT TOOK PLACE ON THAT DAY.

CHAPTER 10: GOING WEST

As the kids traveled back to their time, they thought about what they'd just seen on their adventure.

"Even with the purchase doubling the size of the country at the time, the United States still didn't have all the land it has today," Sam said.

"But it was the beginning of westward expansion," Mia replied. She remembered learning about Americans' movement to the west in the 1800s.

"Wow," Ben said. "Because of the Louisiana Purchase, we have the country we have today!"

IN 1803, JEFFERSON ASKED CONGRESS FOR PERMISSION TO SEND EXPLORERS ACROSS THE LOUISIANA TERRITORY TO THE PACIFIC OCEAN. MERIWETHER LEWIS AND WILLIAM CLARK LED THE EXPLORERS.

LEWIS AND CLARK MAPPED AND STUDIED THE COUNTRY'S NEW LAND. THEY ALSO MADE CONTACT WITH NATIVE AMERICAN PEOPLE THERE. TEAM TIME MACHINE WENT ALONG TOO!

GLOSSARY

acquire: to get as one's own

boundary: something that marks the limit of an area or place

celebration: a time to show happiness for an event through activities such as eating or music

commerce: the large-scale buying and selling of goods and services

Constitution: the basic laws by which the United States is governed

draft: a piece of writing before its completion

emperor: a man who rules an empire, which is a group of regions under one government

minister: an official representing their government in a foreign country

negotiation: the act of coming to an agreement

permission: the right to do something given by someone who has the power to decide if it will be allowed

revolution: a movement to overthrow an established government

treaty: an agreement between countries

FOR MORE INFORMATION

BOOKS

Blashfield, Jean F. *The Amazing Lewis and Clark Expedition.* North Mankato, MN: Capstone Press, 2018.

Rowell, Rebecca. *The Louisiana Purchase.* North Mankato, MN: Core Library, 2017.

Yasuda, Anita. *The Louisiana Purchase Through the Eyes of Thomas Jefferson.* North Mankato, MN: Abdo Publishing, 2016.

WEBSITES

Louisiana Purchase
www.ducksters.com/history/westward_expansion/louisiana_purchase.php
Find out more about the Louisiana Purchase.

Louisiana Purchase: Primary Documents in American History
guides.loc.gov/louisiana-purchase
Take a look at some of the documents from the Louisiana Purchase.

INDEX